# MARJORIE HARRIS
# FAVORITE
# ANNUALS

*Photographs by* **PADDY WALES**

 HarperCollins*Publishers*Ltd

MARJORIE HARRIS FAVORITE ANNUALS
Copyright © 1994 by Marjorie Harris. Photographs © 1994 by Paddy Wales.
No part of this book may be used or reproduced in any manner whatsoever without prior written permission except in the case of brief quotations embodied in reviews. For information address HarperCollins Publishers Ltd, Suite 2900, Hazelton Lanes, 55 Avenue Road, Toronto, Canada M5R 3L2.

First Edition

**Canadian Cataloguing in Publication Data**

Harris, Marjorie
    Marjorie Harris favorite annuals

ISBN 0-00-255404-6 (bound)
ISBN 0-00-638035-2 (pbk.)

1. Annuals (Plants) – Canada. 2. Flower gardening – Canada. I. Title. II. Title: Favorite annuals.

SB422.H37 1994    635.9'312'0971    C94-930697-5

94 95 96 97 98 99 ❖ RRD 10 9 8 7 6 5 4 3 2 1

Printed and bound in Mexico

*Design:* Andrew Smith
*Page layout and composition:* Joseph Gisini, Andrew Smith Graphics, Inc.
*Editing:* Barbara Schon

## ACKNOWLEDGEMENTS

Thanks go to Jacqueline Rogers, who does such a splendid job of research; to Barbara Schon for her care in editing; to Maya Mavjee, who provided the gentle cheerleading; to Tom Thomson, Chief Horticulturist at Humber Nurseries, for reading the manuscript; and to Andrew Smith and Joseph Gisini, who are such marvellous book designers.

Thanks, too, to the wonderful gardeners who allowed us into their gardens: UBC Botanical Gardens; VanDusen Botanical Garden; Park & Tilford Gardens; Mr. and Mrs. W. L. Sauders; Kathy Leishman; Peter and Patricia Wright; John and Sally Woods; Glen Patterson; Pamela Frost; Audrey Litherland; City of Vancouver (Stanley Park); Municipality of West Vancouver.

Thanks to these gardeners for such good ideas: Juliet Mannock, Amanda McConnell, Joan Brink, Thomas Hobbs, Audrey Litherland, Naomi Mann, Barbara Mason, Valerie Pfeiffer and, of course, Paddy Wales, who always has good ideas.

COVER: *Viola labradorica*

# *Contents*

# *Annuals*

Annuals bring freshness and light to the garden. Though I'm not wild about all-annual gardens, a garden without them is a poor place. It is the mix of perennials, shrubs and annuals that gives a garden a settled quality.

The usefulness of annuals is enormous even in the most established of gardens. They give immediate color, whereas it often takes perennials a few years to really shine. They can be used between perennials to fill in while they are becoming mature, to cover up the spaces left when bulb foliage starts to rot, or next to new shrubs. And they are the ultimate container plants.

Because seeds are cheap, it is possible to experiment with all sorts of new and interesting plants. Annuals mean more than petunias and impatiens, however worthy both these plants are. With annuals you can afford to have drifts of color and combinations of shape and size. There is one rule with annuals never to be broken—never, ever plant them in soldier-like rows.

Let annuals bloom in succession; grow them as a standard (pruned to a single stem) such as a lantana or fuchsia; or use them as edging for border plants or as vivid ground covers.

The ones I've chosen here are heavy on my favorite colors—blues, whites, pinks and yellows. I assume people know that petunias are great plants—they just aren't my favorite. There are lots of really marvellous new cultivars, so you don't have to put up with anything dull. Once petunias have had a first flowering, whack them back enough to take off all the spent blooms. They will live to bloom again.

*Cleome spinosa*

I'm also assuming that everyone will include impatiens in their garden. These indispensable annuals add a glow to shady corners of borders or decks.

Annuals complete their life cycle in one year. They are born, grow up, produce seed, then die. The profuse flowering of annuals is not simply to give great pleasure but to produce a mass of seeds to ensure its survival. Here are some facts to help you make your selections:

❧ Annual seeds are either standards or hybrids. With *standards*, pollination has occurred naturally and the seeds will come true, as the saying goes—they will look exactly like the parents. Collect seeds on a dry day in the autumn when the seeds look desiccated but are still on the plant. Store them in labelled envelopes in a jar.

❧ With *hybrids*, pollination between selected parents has been done by hand—these seeds will revert to one parent, usually the least interesting.

❧ When you buy seeds, the differing depths or times of bloom on the package instructions have to do with regional differences. Everything is approximate and depends on the amount of light and exposure available.

❧ **Hardy** annuals are always native to temperate zones, don't require heat to germinate and can be seeded directly into the garden. They often self-seed, so they keep popping up year after year, giving the impression that they might be perennial. Excellent for naturalizing. Many of them can be planted in autumn close enough to the first frost that they won't get a chance to germinate. Nothing needs to be done in spring except to thin them out. They bloom in summer, set seed and overwinter to sprout in succeeding springs. Second sowing of seeds will produce blooms later in the year.

❧ **Half-hardy** are those annual seeds that can be planted in place in spring before the weather gets hot—they like cool, not cold, weather. But a few frosts, no matter how light, will do them in. Most of the popular annuals fall into this category and they need a bit more care. They need heat to germinate. Seeds can be sown indoors, or outside when the weather gets warm enough.

❧ **Tender** annuals will croak if they get hit with frost and must be started indoors early in spring or planted outdoors when there's absolutely no danger of frost and the soil is warm to the touch.

## SOME TIPS ABOUT PLANTING ANNUAL SEEDS

❧ Fine seeds generally should be started indoors, since it's hard for them to compete with aggressive weeds that might be lurking in the soil. There's also a risk of being washed away by heavy spring rains.

❧ For plants that hate to be transplanted, start the seeds in peat pots or Jiffy-7 pots. Plant pot and all when the seedlings reach the proper size.

❧ Clean flats and pots thoroughly before using with a few tablespoons of household bleach in a gallon of water (30 mL/4 L).

*Lobelia* 'Crystal Palace'

🌿 **To prepare new beds:** Dig the soil to at least 1 foot (30 cm), and even more if you have the energy. Break up any clods and rake the soil even; water. Broadcast the seed over the bed, then cover with finely sifted soil. Water thoroughly with a mister.

🌿 Plant each seed as deep as the seed at its thickest spot and at the same distance apart.

🌿 Don't let the bed dry out until you start seeing growth. Once germination has taken place, cut back to watering deeply once a week—this encourages deep roots. Keep weeded, and watch out for slugs.

🌿 Since most seeds produce flowers within 12 weeks of sowing, plan your garden with this in mind.

🌿 **Annuals to plant in place:** Blue lace flower, larkspur, lavatera, love-in-a-mist, mignonette, nasturtium, nolana, phlox, California and Shirley poppies, portulaca, sweet pea, creeping zinnia.

🌿 **Plant in fall for spring bloom:** Candytuft, celosia, cornflower, coreopsis, cosmos, kochia, larkspur, nicotiana, annual poppies, portulaca, salvia, spider flower, spurge, sweet alyssum, sweet pea.

Sow just before a killer frost so they won't germinate before freezing. Always sow slightly deeper than what's recommended for spring planting.

🌿 **Seeds needing dark to germinate:** Bachelor's-button, calendula, forget-me-not, gazania, larkspur, nasturtium, nemesia, pansy, penstemon, periwinkle, phlox, sweet pea, verbena.

❧ **Annuals for shade:** *Impatiens,* the most familiar of all annuals can grow in both sun *and* shade. I love pots of white ones to glow at night. And always have them in out-of-the-way corners to perk things up. There's no substitute. But I'm not a big fan of the neon pinks and salmons—nothing but drifts of these plants is gagging. Others for shade: begonia, browallia, cleome, coleus, fuschia, lobelia, monkey flower and nicotiana.

❧ **Half-shade:** All of the above plus ageratum, China aster, balsam, black-eyed Susan vine, dianthus, dusty-miller, forget-me-not, pansy, periwinkle, salvia and sweet alyssum.

❧ **Dry sites:** African daisy, amaranthus, celosia, dusty-miller, globe amaranth, petunia, portulaca, spider flower, statice, strawflower and zinnia.

❧ **Annuals for cutting:** Always plant extra seeds so you have flowers for cutting. Once a flower is in the garden I figure that's where it's supposed to stay. Many years ago I put in a cutting border in the Jardin des Refusés, which is where I put anything I can't cope with elsewhere in the garden. This mishmash of flowers is not organized, so I feel quite free to cut things for indoors.

Besides those mentioned in the listings, these plants make splendid bouquets: baby's-breath, bachelor's-buttons, blue lace flower, butterfly flower, cosmos in all colors, dahlias, pot marigold, sweet peas, zinnias.

❧ **Annuals for drying:** Suitable plants are identified in the listings. It's surprising what you can dry. Cut the plants just before or just after the buds have opened. Hang them upside down in a cool, dark spot with good air circulation, and in a few weeks they'll be ready to use. Delphinium and larkspurs; peony and statice; all the everlasting flowers such as *Helichrysum bracteatum* and *Helipterum,* both strawflower; globe amaranth, lunaria and many of the annual grasses will do you proud.

❧ **Buying Annuals from the Nursery:** Try to choose compact plants with good foliage without any little whiteflies or mites floating around them. Check to make sure they aren't overly potbound.

## PLANTING

I always place the potted plants around the garden so I get a feel for how they will disport themselves. This is a lot of fun, and you develop a real knack after a few years of being able to visualize just how big they'll get and how much space they will take up. I tend to put annuals closer together than is recommended because I like to get a really good display from them as quickly as possible. But you always run the risk of damaging them by doing this. Start by following the rules, then break them.

❧ Plant very early in the morning, late in the afternoon, or on a cool cloudy day.

⚜ Always treat nursery-grown plants with great care—they shouldn't sit around in a hot car or be left out in the sun. Give them a soak in tepid water before you plant.

⚜ Prepare a large enough hole to take the root system and extra width. Don't cheat, and the plants will reward you by being extra-healthy. Water the hole first, let drain, then pop the plant into place. Water again.

⚜ At the end of the season, pull out all your annuals and put any healthy corpses into the compost to break down over winter and provide new food next year.

⚜ Tender perennials can be used as houseplants over the winter.

## CONTAINERS

Container planting is one of the most irresistible forms of gardening. Don't be rigid about just having pots on a deck or in some kind of prissy arrangement. Use them all over the garden wherever you need a splash of color.

Annuals seem designed for containers. But don't get ditzy little ones; make sure they are a sensible size. Too many small ones scattered about give a cluttered look to the garden, and the plants will have to be watered constantly. Use pots that are more than a foot (30 cm) wide and as deep. They hold more plants and don't need watering as often.

Good drainage is important; make a hole in the bottom if there isn't one. Decide where you want a large container before you fill it up. Moving them around is a pain. Set the plants you want in them loosely and figure out what kind of placement you're aiming for. All plants have a face, or good side, and look for it when you are placing them.

The planting medium is important. Since roots have to put up with what are clearly stress conditions under strict confinement, be careful what's used. Ordinary garden soil probably isn't a good idea. It may get compacted and harm delicate annual roots. But you can still make your own mix. Dump the following onto a big piece of plastic and stir it up: one-third potting soil, one-third sphagnum moss and one-third horticultural sand. This kind of lightweight mix is also good for containers on balconies and roof gardens.

⚜ Paint the insides of the containers with latex paint to keep the soil from drying out as rapidly. Or try a water-based urethane. Just be sure it isn't an oil-based paint or you will shorten the life of the plant.

⚜ Arrange the plants so that the edges of the container will be concealed.

⚜ The color in pots is going to be very concentrated, so remember that when putting white annuals in with other colors the tones will shift slightly.

⚜ Mass containers—a minimum of three or four—in groups like a miniature landscape. Move them around to get different effects as the season wears on.

## MAINTENANCE

❧ Water regularly in dreadfully hot weather, even if it's once or twice a day. Stick your finger in to the first joint: if it's dry, water.

❧ Fertilize by mixing up a cup (250 mL) of compost or manure to a gallon (4 L) of water and let it sit for a day before adding to the containers every few weeks. Or use a commercial seaweed formula at half strength.

❧ Deadhead, to keep plants neat and from setting seed so they'll flower right up to the first frost. Collect faded blossoms each day and use little Japanese bonsai scissors to nick off dead heads or tough stems.

❧ **Annuals for containers:** Any form of the scented or ivy-leaved geranium (really pelargoniums) available in glorious shades of pink and white. They give a wonderful feeling of Mediterranean heat and light.

Almost any plant mentioned in this book is an excellent pot plant. Here are a few others you might also consider: ageratum, begonia, blue-eyed African daisy, Swan River daisy, gazania; any of the plants called dusty-miller.

❧ Mix annuals with perennials such as lilies, shrubs, trees, even vines.

❧ **Annual vines:** They will quickly cover an ugly garage or pole. They provide a green wall in one season, giving you a chance to put in slower-growing vines, which often take three or four years.

❧ Use them to trail through areas you want covered up, or dripping down off the edges of an urn or container. Train them up from a windowbox or pot around a balcony or deck to give a glorious filtered shade.

*Papaver somniferum*

# *Borago officinalis*

FAMILY NAME: *Boraginaceae*
PHOTOGRAPHED IN THE GARDEN OF: Kathy Leishman

I n the world of textures, borage is at the top of the heap. The fuzzy gray-green leaves and the brilliant cobalt flowers are a giant plus. I've given up trying to organize borage; it's like an unruly child. It will self-seed wherever it pleases. It flops over other plants but gently so, making its very own aesthetic arrangements with them.

If you want to attract bees to the garden, borage is a great seducer. But this is a sun-loving plant, and it won't produce flowers unless it has lots of sun. The nodding pendulous, long-stalked blue flowers of *B. officinalis* are cupped at the centre to produce a star-shaped bloom. The hairy, rather prickly surface makes it an uncomfortable plant to try to pull out if it pops up where it's not wanted. The name may come from the Latin *burra,*

*Borago officinalis*

❧ This sun-loving, easy-to-grow plant likes rich soil that's well fertilized with manure and compost. Keep the soil fairly loose and well mulched to hold moisture. And give the plant lots of room. Having said that, it's also prepared to put up with poor situations and is somewhat drought tolerant—it won't take up as much room as if you treat it well.

❧ Start seeds indoors or spread them where you want them in early spring. Once the plant establishes itself, it will continue to self-seed.

❧ Borage is said to increase the resistance to disease and pests of any neighboring plants.

❧ Self-seeding is the most practical way of propagating them.

meaning rough, probably alluding to stems and foliage of this rough, hairy plant. In Europe borage is a common wild plant, which you can see all over sun-drenched hillsides. It has naturalized in North America. But you must have space for this annual, which tumbles about. It can cover a 4 foot (1.2 m) area and grows from 1' – 1½' (30 cm – 45 cm).

The plant was once a favorite of herbalists as a source of courage and emotional strength, a plant to dispel gloom and melancholy. It's certain to perk up any part of a sunny border or soften hard edges of paths. Because it's constantly in flower you have months of reliable color when you're putting combinations together. That's one reason I have it with *Gaura lindheimeri*, a tall wiry perennial with small white to pink flowers. They both have enormously long bloom periods. And the contrast between erect and droopy, elegance and coarseness, is delightful. Borage is a good plant with artemisias—both having gray foliage. Use it in pots so that you can move it around to the sunniest parts of the garden.

Borage flowers are wonderful in cooking. In this case the clear blue of the flowers is what counts, according to photographer Paddy Wales. She thinks it looks stunning on a fruit flan with kiwis and blueberries. A garden picture becomes a picture on a plate. The taste, by the way, is somewhat like cucumber. And the leaves can be cooked the same way as spinach. The flowers can be candied, or added as a garnish and flavour to Pimm's No. 1 Cup.

## OTHER SPECIES & CULTIVARS

*B. laxiflora*, from Corsica, excellent for the rock garden or front of the border. This decorative hardy perennial grows 1½' – 2' (45 cm – 60 cm); zone 3.

# *Browallia*

FAMILY NAME: *Solanaceae*
PHOTOGRAPHED IN THE GARDEN OF: Paddy Wales

Blue flowers have a special place in my heart. I mass browallias into a huge blue-and-white Chinese pot and set it out in a slightly shady corner on the deck. This captivating plant will cope with light shade and just doesn't seem to quit flowering from June to frost. It combines well with low-growing lobelias tumbling out the side of the pot.

But it doesn't stop there. It's possible to bring it indoors for the winter, where it will continue flowering. Cut back in autumn and repot. To help it adjust to indoor temps, start bringing it in when nights are getting cold and before you've turned on the furnace, then put it out again during the day. Repeat this until the plant has hardened itself to indoor life. Keep it in the sunniest spot for reblooming.

The bright blue flowers (also violet and pure white, depending on the species) are up to 2 inches (5 cm) across. The form is extremely elegant, with well-branched wiry stems and almost bushy foliage. They grow from 8" – 14" (20 cm – 30 cm) high and will spread 1 foot (30 cm). The star-like blooms have five petals with one-sided racemes. The leaves are bright green, pointy at each end with veins beneath.

There are six species in a genus that's native to South America and the West Indies. The most common ones used outside are *B. americana*, *B. speciosa*, and their cultivars. *B. speciosa* (*speciosa* means showy) is a native of Colombia, where it can reach 5 feet (1.5 m), and the velvet blooms look a little like the trumpet of a petunia. It grows to 12" – 14" (30 cm – 40 cm) with the same spread. This half-hardy annual grows in a low-spreading, almost shrubby manner. There are blue, white and lavender forms. The stalks are hairless.

Though browallia can take a lot of abuse, they can't take very high temperatures, being left in direct sunlight or being allowed to go completely dry. Browallia is one of those plants that prefers to be potbound. It thrives when its roots are crowded comfortably inside a container. This is a terrific plant for baskets or containers. Plant one pot intensively and set it in the garden near a large hosta. 'White Bell', with compact pure white flowers, is excellent for pots, and 'Blue Troll' for hanging baskets.

*Browallia speciosa*

In the warmest areas it will self-sow in very protected sites. If you have a children's garden, this would be an easy one for them to start with. Put browallias together with *Calamintha*, a herb with pink to lilac flowers. The darker quality of the browallias seems to bring out the best in the calaminthas.

❧ Browallias definitely need some shade—too much sun and the blooms get bleached—and they must have moist, but not wet, well-drained soil. Don't overwater or overfertilize, or all you'll get is a pile of foliage. Browallias will grow in almost anything, including very poor dry soil, but they'll be much smaller. If you add lots of organic matter they will be quite lush.

❧ Set nursery-grown plants about 10 inches (25 cm) apart. As the plants reach 4 inches (10 cm), pinch them back to make them bushier and more floriferous.

❧ Easy to grow from seed, browallias bloom about three months after germinating. Start indoors eight weeks before the last frost. Germination should take about 14 to 21 days if seeds are exposed to light.

❧ Pinch back to maintain shape and encourage flowering.

❧ This plant likes humidity, so mist it regularly. This, of course, is a necessity if you bring the plant indoors.

❧ The most common problem is black spot disease. Remove the affected leaves and get them out of the garden. Don't put them in the compost.

## OTHER SPECIES & CULTIVARS

*B. speciosa* grows 8" – 15" (20 cm – 38 cm) high. The flowers are 2 inches (5 cm) wide on short stalks. This is a good cut flower and lasts well in water.

'Blue Bells' has violet blue flowers.

'Major' has dark blue flowers.

*B. viscosa* is a floriferous plant that grows 12" – 20" (30 cm – 50 cm) high. The flowers are ¾ inch (2 cm), in a violet blue with a white eye.

'Alba' has white flowers.

'Compacta' is a low-growing form.

# Cleome spinosa

FAMILY NAME: *Capparaceae*
PHOTOGRAPHED IN: University of British Columbia Botanical Garden

*Cleome spinosa*

My first sighting of a cleome, with its enormous spidery blooms and unbelievable height, brought me literally to a halt. I saw it in a public garden in Toronto a few years ago, and I stopped my car and got out. Popular half a century ago, it slowly sank out of public favor for some peculiar reason, then out of sight. Horticulturists brought it back in Europe and we followed soon after here in North America.

Cleomes are well named—spider plants. These South American natives look so exotic, with huge stamens wafting about in the breeze, and have an evocative strong scent. The weirdness of the dangling stamens and the sheer height make this an audacious plant, ideal as a show stopper in a large group or mixed with other plants its own size. The hairy, spiny stems are erect and stiff enough to never need staking—ergo, it's an ideal plant for rearguard action in the border.

Of the 200 species in this tropical genus, only one is ordinarily cultivated for the garden. Cleomes can reach 6 feet (2 m) in ideal situations, but they normally reach 3' – 4' (1 m – 1.2 m). The genus consists of annuals and a few evergreen shrubs. The leaves are compound, with three to seven leaflets. Then there are the huge round flower heads with narrow petals and those curious long stamens.

*C. hasslerana* (syn. *C. arborea, C. gigantea, C. spinosa*) is a species from Brazil and Argentina. It's a half-hardy annual that grows to a fair height, 3' – 5' (1 m – 1.5 m) with a spread of 18 inches (45 cm). Sticky, almost thorny stems rise from the base of the stems. Most hybrids come from this species.

Cleomes bloom from summer until frost strikes them dead. The flowers open up in succession over the summer and are only fully alive in the evening. They come in good strong tones of pink, purple, yellow and white. Once the flowering is over they develop huge languorous-looking seedpods, which stick out on wiry stems and are almost as ornamental as the flowers. Plant them near roses that have reached the same height, as an amusing foil.

### OTHER SPECIES & CULTIVARS

*C. hasslerana* (syn. *C. arborea, C. gigantea, C. spinosa*):
'Colour Fountain Mixed' is a good screening plant; scented pink, rose, lilac, purple and white flowers; grows to 3½ feet (1 m). 'Cherry Queen', carmine; 'Helen Campbell' is one of the best, and most pure white; 'Pink Queen'; 'Violet Queen'.

*C. lutea* is an American native that reaches 3½ feet (1 m).

# *Cosmos bipinnatus*

FAMILY NAME: *Compositae*
PHOTOGRAPHED IN THE GARDEN OF: Paddy Wales

W hen we bought our house in 1968, the back garden was nearly filled with weeds, thorns and a lot of other equally intimidating plants. The only space left for anything else was filled with cosmos. They struggled on magnificently, refusing to be choked out by any living thing. In late summer I see gardens all around me that are almost completely taken over by cosmos. The rich colors, lacy foliage and wonderful daisy-like flowers are always enchanting.

I have cosmos planted near some old-fashioned rugosa roses to add color when they are past their prime and with other tall slim plants such as *Boltonia asteroides*, a wonderful daisy-like giant that grows to 7 feet (2 m) and

*Cosmos bipinnatus*

*Cosmos bipinnatus*

*Rudbeckia nitida* 'Herbstonne', the same height in a brilliant yellow. Autumn is the time to have these combinations, and this is a particularly good one. If you have any sort of wild area in your garden that can be allowed to self-sow, add cosmos to the mix.

Until 1895 only white, pink and crimson forms of *C. bipinnatus* were available. In 1896 *C. sulphureus* was introduced and hybridization began in earnest. Today there are many very good ones in a wide range of clear colors. *C. bipinnatus* is a native of Mexico, and there are 20 species in the genus. It has large-petalled flowers with delicate-looking foliage and blooms almost continuously throughout the summer. It has long stems and grows $3\frac{1}{2}' - 6\frac{1}{2}'$ (1 m – 2 m) high. This is the workhorse of the annual garden. It isn't bothered by heat and it comes on early and fast. The colors range from white to candy stripes.

'Sensation' hybrids grow to a maximum of $3\frac{1}{2}$ feet (1 m) and should be spaced 3 feet (1 m) apart. Pinch back early in the season for fuller growth. 'Candy Stripe' has white petals striped with crimson; grows to 1 foot (30 cm).

'Sonata' is pure white with a yellow centre; grows to 2 feet (60 cm).

Cosmos have an Old World quality to them that makes them suitable for a traditional cottage garden. They not only give color to a border but also add texture with the filigree foliage and crushed-velvet quality of the bloom. They're useful next to perennials that die in August and September, and are a much-needed addition to any spaces between large perennials such as asters and phlox.

## PLANTING & MAINTENANCE TIPS

❧ Don't make the soil too rich for this drudgery-loving plant or it will become leggy without a lot of flowers. The best soil is on the sandy side.

❧ Loves the sun but will take a bit of shade as well. Can tolerate some drought.

❧ Nip back in late spring for a much bushier plant.

❧ Seeds can be sown in spring outdoors once there's no danger of frost. Or sow indoors three to four weeks before the last frost. Plant seedlings 1 foot (30 cm) apart.

❧ If you don't deadhead it will self-seed right back to the original pinks and magentas.

❧ The seeds of white cosmos should be started indoors rather than trying to sow them in place outside.

❧ This genus is completely pest-free.

## OTHER SPECIES & CULTIVARS

*C. atrosanguineus*, black cosmos, looks like a big dahlia; has scented flowers that aren't black so much as a deep, deep maroon. Tubers can be lifted and stored over the winter. Needs sun and moist soil. This is a container plant highly recommended by Penelope Hobhouse, the great English garden writer. A perennial from zone 7.

*C. sulphureus* is shorter than the other species at 6 feet (2 m). The colors are much richer in red, yellow or orange; often has double flowers 2½ inches (6 cm) across. The foliage is rather bushy though still fairly delicate.

'Diablo' grows only 1½ feet (45 cm); compact form; color ranges from yellow to orange to red.

'Klondyke' strain includes:

'Ladybird Mixed', 10 inches (25 cm) high with with tangerine and yellow semi-double flowers; 'Lemon Twist', 2' – 2½' (60 cm – 75 cm) high, with grapefruit yellow flowers good for cutting; 'Sunny Gold', 14" – 18" (35 cm – 45 cm); and 'Sunny Red', 1 foot (30 cm).

# *Echium vulgare* 'Blue Bedder'

FAMILY NAME: *Boraginaceae*
PHOTOGRAPHED IN THE GARDEN OF: Kathy Leishman

I first saw this plant in the south of France and stood in awe before the dazzling silver foliage and bright blue spikes of flowers. It seemed to be everywhere holding up hillsides or as stunning specimens as the anchor of simple garden borders. This is usually a biennial, which means you plant one year, it forms roots and leaves, and the second year it blooms. The name comes from Greek *echis*, meaning viper, because of the corolla that projects outward like a snake's head.

*E. vulgare*, viper's bugloss, reaches 1' – 3' (30 cm – 1 m) in height and has cup-shaped flowers of white, pink, blue or purple. The hairy leaves are narrow, gray-green and lance-shaped. In its natural European habitat it can grow in mountains at 6,000 feet (1800 m), but it's equally at home by the sea. This is a biennial grown as an annual, which means it has to be sown early to bloom the first year. It grows quite quickly.

*E. v.* 'Blue Bedder' has glorious complex blue spike-like flower clusters. It creates a superb blue tapestry background to a sunny part of the garden. *E. v.* 'T & M Dwarf Mixed' grows to 1 foot (30 cm); rose, pink and light blue are among its many colors.

## PLANTING & MAINTENANCE TIPS

❧ Plant in full sun in average soil; overly rich soil will produce far too much foliage. Can tolerate dry soil with excellent drainage. Space plants 10" – 15" (25 cm – 38 cm) apart.

❧ Sow seeds in early spring after the last frost. Or start seeds indoors eight or nine weeks before last frost. Seeds germinate at 60 – 65°F (15 – 18°C). Be sure to harden seedlings off by putting them outdoors during the day and bringing them in at night until the temperatures are steadily warm. Or put them in a cold frame for a few weeks.

❧ In the right site, echium will self-sow.

*Echium vulgare* 'Blue Bedder'

Every year around April 15 one of my hortbuddies flings Epsom salts, which acts as a fungicide, around the soil near old roses and adds some new topsoil to which she had added a mix of echium, candytuft and alyssum seeds. She ends up with a carpet of wonderful flowers that grow up just enough to hide the bottoms of the roses.

This is a good plant to use in conjunction with strawberry plants. They complement each other.

## OTHER SPECIES & CULTIVARS

*E. lycopsis* (*E. plantagineum*) has rich purple, blue, mauve and violet flowers above broad leaves covered with white hairs. Grows to 3 feet (1 m).

*E. fastuosum*, Pride of Madeira, is a tender biennial; has long spikes of blue-purple flowers in May and June; in warm zones it's evergreen with gray-green leaves. Grows 5' – 6½' (1.5 m – 2 m). Needs a sunny spot out of the wind.

# *Felicia amelloides*

FAMILY NAME: *Compositae*
PHOTOGRAPHED IN THE GARDEN OF: Paddy Wales

My very first love of a flower was for daisies, and now I'm instinctively drawn to any plant with even vaguely similar starry, rayed blossoms. Felicias qualify perfectly. There are about 50 species in this genus, all native to South Africa and Ethiopia. They need long, hot summers to do well. It's worth trying this plant because it flowers almost continuously from June to October and is a quick-growing semi-prostrate plant, which makes it great in a pot all by itself.

*F. amelloides* (syn. *F. capensis*), blue Marguerite or blue daisy, is a sub-shrub in South Africa and won't overwinter in North America. This annual needs full sun and lots of pinching back to make it bushier. The more it's pinched back, the more it will flower as well. Do this once for sure, and possibly twice, early in the season. This species is botanically related to asters. One of the more charming habits of its blossoms is to turn in on themselves when the weather becomes overcast. You can watch them open up right

*Felicia amelloides*

❧ Felicias will not flower unless they get full sun. Though they aren't fussy about soil, it should be well drained and never overwatered. You can add compost to it as the season rolls along. In containers and hanging baskets use well-drained sandy soil.

❧ In places with hot summers, sow indoors eight weeks before last frost and transplant outdoors in May; in cool-summer areas sow outdoors in spring with other hardy annuals. Space felicias 6 inches (15 cm) apart. Pinch back when it reaches a few inches (centimetres) high from the main stem. Then pinch the lateral growth once or twice.

before your eyes when the sun returns. The intense blue blooms, with yellow centres, are ¾ inch (2 cm) wide on 12 inch (30 cm) wiry stems.

Felicias flop about enough for windowboxes or balcony planters, yet they are bushy and compact so they won't become a dreary mess. They grow quickly, spreading to almost 2½ feet (75 cm). The opposite leaves are either elongated or rounded. They make a handsome background for the single little daisy-like flower at the end of each stem.

It's possible to let a few of these plants spread about in a rough area. But I like adding them to borders filled with perennials. The scale is just right for the front of a border to soften edges and give a romantic look.

One splendid gardener of my acquaintance uses felicias in a stone urn. He trains it slightly upwards to make an even more graceful mass. He also has it with heliotrope and several lobelias, white nicotina and pale pink pelargoniums (annual geraniums), letting it spill out over decks and porches.

I have felicias with *Marrubium*, horehound, and *Helichrysum petiolatum* in pots. The contrast between the gray foliage and the blue and green of the felicias has a serene aura.

## OTHER SPECIES & CULTIVARS

*F. bergerana*, kingfisher daisy, grows to 6" – 8" (15 cm – 20 cm) and forms mats of blue flowers over gray foliage. Very good for edging and containers. Sterile flowers, yellow to black centres and blue rays.

*F. hispida* is similar to *amelloides* and considered a better form because it has larger and even more prolific sky blue flowers. Bristly, elongated foliage grows to 3 feet (1 m).

*F. tenella*, an annual species with thin pointy leaves covered in silky hairs. Single small terminal flowers; grows 12" – 15" (30 cm – 38 cm).

# *Helichrysum petiolatum*

FAMILY NAME: *Compositae*
PHOTOGRAPHED IN THE GARDEN OF: Audrey Litherland

*Helichrysum petiolatum*

This is my most valuable annual, and every year I try to think of new ways to use it. It fits in everywhere with its velvety rounded leaves and graceful spread outward from the woody centre. The name, from the Greek *helios*, sun, and *chrysos*, golden, refers to the everlasting flower in the daisy family. The part of the genus I like best, though, has only a marginally interesting bloom. It's for the glorious foliage that I need this plant.

*H. petiolatum* is native to South Africa and can grow up to 2 feet (60 cm), almost like a subshrub, and stretch 3 feet (1 m). The felty silver stems have leaves 1 inch (2.5 cm) long. It grows remarkably fast. 'Limelight' is a pale chartreuse and will take a bit of shade. 'Variegatum' is creamy. Both are interesting variations if you can find them.

I have helichrysums insinuating themselves near a low-growing Japanese maple, *Acer palmatum* 'Dissectum Atropurpureum'—they mingle with each other—and a *Ruta graveolens* 'Curly Girl' lounges nearby. Another dynamite foliage combination is with *Perilla frutescens*, a huge purple-leaved herb with curly edges on the leaves that is both commanding in itself and a good plant for a foliage area. Helichrysums also look good with the slim but stiff stems of *Physostegia*, obedient plant.

In pots, helichrysums are nonpareil. I use them with both perennials and annuals; with masses of trailing lobelia—the darker the better for contrast; with nemesias; with marguerites; with ivy-leaved geraniums (pelargoniums).

To prepare pots, start with the helichrysum—one plant to a pot or you'll find that you have too much—then start adding the other plants. Make sure the helichrysum can angle itself over the side or be flat up against a wall. In the latter position it can be trained to almost look like a climber.

The great English garden writer Christopher Lloyd suggests the following: put a cane in the soil near the middle of the plant and tie a shoot to this. As the shoot grows, keep on clipping it to the cane with stem ties. This way, he says, it will grow 3' – 4' (1 m – 1.2 m) tall and will make horizontal side branches like a little tree.

I have never been able to overwinter helichrysums. I have a great big terracotta pot with a *Laurus nobilis,* bay laurel; and a marjoram usually enhanced with at least one helichrysum. Then I add summer-flowering bulbs for a smattering of color. Everything stands up to the rigors of indoor life except the helichrysum. It goes along just fine until January, then one day it croaks.

## PLANTING & MAINTENANCE TIPS

❧ Must have sun. It flops about in my garden because it gets barely enough (just about six hours a day). This plant will take both lots of heat and drought once it's established. Any soil, as long as it isn't too wet. A lot of moisture will make *H. petiolatum* and *H. angustifolium* rot from the centre and look terrible. Keep them trimmed so they stay shapely by cutting off the rather dull little flowers.

❧ Add lots of compost to the soil around these plants.

❧ Propagate from cuttings in early autumn. Overwinter them in a cool place in the same pots they sprout roots in.

## OTHER SPECIES & CULTIVARS

*H. italicum* (syn. *H. angustifolium*), curry plant, from southern Europe, is worth having just to brush by and take a whiff of regularly—smells just like curry. An almost white-silver crowded foliage with tiny yellow flowers. Ideal for pots. Grows to 1 foot (30 cm) high. Can be overwintered indoors if you water it regularly. Grows to 2 feet (60 cm).

# *Heliotropium arborescens*

FAMILY NAME: *Boraginaceae*
PHOTOGRAPHED IN THE GARDEN OF: Glen Patterson

This is one of those old cottage garden type of plants. It has a wonderful scent and comes in incredible colors—good enough to attract bees and butterflies to the garden. In herbal medicine it was used as an astringent. In European countries it's still grown to use in perfumes. Victorians called it cherry-pie because of the slight fragrance of vanilla.

There are more than 250 species in the genus *Heliotropium*, most of which are found in warm areas. *Helios* is Greek for sun; *trope*, turning. Heliotropism is a tendency some plants have of turning towards the sun. The flowers have five petals, and the rounded form makes it an easy plant to use. It has coarse, almost corrugated foliage with alternate leaves that are 3 inches (7.5 cm) long. The plant reaches $1\frac{1}{2}'$ – 3' (45 cm – 1.2 m) with a

*Heliotropium arborescens*

❧ Plant in full sun. In extremely warm areas, give the plants some shade from afternoon sun. Needs a rich, moist soil with lots of compost or manure added.

❧ Take cuttings in September for plants to winter indoors. Root them in half peat moss and half sand.

❧ Sow seeds in spring in ordinary soil. Germination can take three weeks. Set out in the garden two to three weeks after the last frost. Set out plants 8" – 10" (20 cm – 25 cm) apart.

❧ Keep deadheading the flowers. And cut back after the first flush has passed.

❧ Will succumb to rot if put into a damp area.

spread of 1' – 2½' (30 cm – 75 cm).

Because of the scent it's important to grow heliotropes where the odor can travel through windows or to a nearby seating area. I have them near the deck along with *Lavatera* 'Mont Blanc'. This is a rather harsh white-purple-blue combination that I find satisfying since everything around is soft grays, yellows and pinks. It's not to everyone's taste.

One of the gardeners I admire says she always buys about eight plants, never knowing beforehand where she's going to put them, and searches out holes for them. Some of the combinations look fairly weird, but she's will-ing to move things around if it doesn't work. She puts heliotrope with *Salvia viridis* (*S. horminum*), which has transparent wings of blue flowers, and the contrast with deep purple and green is really satisfying. Years ago I gave her *Artemisia pontica*, Roman wormwood, a seriously invasive plant—she was warned and marries it with heliotropes. This is such a good combi-nation that I've stolen it for my own garden.

A spectacular combination is with fuchsias near *Heuchera micrantha* 'Palace Purple'. Put it with *Matthiola incana*, stocks; *Mirabilis jalapa*, four o'clocks; and salvias.

For cut flowers, put heliotropes in water right up to the neck of the blooms for a few hours in a dark place. They'll last much longer this way.

## OTHER SPECIES & CULTIVARS

'Dwarf Marine', 14 inches (35 cm) tall, is ideal for containers and windowboxes because of its compact size.

x 'Hybrid Marine', 18 inches (45 cm) purple fragrant flower with deep green foliage.

x *peruvianum* (syn. *H. arborescens*), 1½' – 2' (45 cm – 60 cm) tall, has a sweet scent and comes in lavender to purple, not always with a white eye. Ideal for a windowbox.

# *Iberis amara*
## 'Giant Hyacinth Flowered'

FAMILY NAME: *Cruciferae*
PHOTOGRAPHED IN THE GARDEN OF: Kathy Leishman

The first seeds I sowed in place were *Iberis umbellata*. For the past twenty-odd years these flowers have been pure joy. They move themselves around the garden in the most enchanting way. Some come up looking almost white with a slight pink cast, some are pale lavenders of no particular distinction. Other years they will favor purple and more silky tones of pink.

I've tried culling the ones I like best, but these plants just do whatever they wish. They pop up in surprising combinations with other plants—usually in combinations I would never have thought of—and form pictures of surprising grace. Just the way nature intended.

*I. amara* (syn *I. coronaria*), rocket candytuft, is a hardy annual that grows to 1 foot (30 cm), and has been cultivated in gardens since the sixteenth century. It has thin lance-shaped leaves 3 inches (7.5 cm) long and spikes of scented glistening white flowers with slightly flat heads. 'Flash Mixed' flowers are white, red, purple, lilac and pink. 'Giant Hyacinth

### PLANTING & MAINTENANCE TIPS

❧ Candytuft makes do with full sun, although they prefer part shade where summers are hot.

❧ They need only ordinary garden soil but must have good drainage since they hate standing around in too much moisture. Will tolerate some drought.

❧ Seeds take 10 to 20 days to germinate.

❧ In areas of mild winters, sow seeds in place in late summer. In areas of cold winters, wait until spring to scatter seeds. Make successive sowings up to mid-June to have blooms right through fall.

❧ Blooms six weeks after germinating. Keep deadheading during the season or shear back after the first bloom. This will keep them coming on until autumn.

❧ Prone to white rust. Pull out diseased plants and get rid of them completely.

*Iberis armara* 'Giant Hyacinth Flowered'

Flowered' has delicate white hyacinth-shaped flowers and grows 15" – 18" (38 cm – 45 cm). 'Pinnacle' is the same size but an even purer white.

Iberises are excellent annuals with shrubs. They seem to be able to disport themselves gracefully around them, fitting in snugly in awkward spots. They are splendid pot plants and mix in well with other annuals and foliage plants such as helichrysums. As a threader through the garden I can't think of a better choice. I have iberises running through a bed of pale blue *Calamintha nepetoides*; white *Physostegia*, obedient plant; and yellow *Alchemilla mollis*, Lady's-mantle.

One hortbuddy collects seedheads in fall, dries them, then goes out in early spring and "baptizes" her entire garden with them to inspire random new combinations. Later, she merely weeds out what's not wanted. She's been using the descendants of the same plant for 25 years. This is a very long-lived annual.

## OTHER SPECIES & CULTIVARS

*I. odorata* is a highly scented species. Native of Crete. Grows 1 foot (30 cm) high.

*I. sempervirens*, perennial candytuft, has deep green evergreen foliage and glaring white flowers. In small drifts this is a terrific plant. It makes a crisp, tailored low hedge for a semi-formal garden. 'Snowflake' is a great mat-forming plant. Grows to 9 inches (22 cm) with a spread of 2 feet (60 cm).

*I. umbellata*, candytuft, is lower-growing than *I. amara* with a mound or dome-shaped flower and it's probably the best known of all. It's not, alas, fragrant, which is about the only disappointing thing about this plant. The flowers are 2 inches (5 cm) across in pink, lilac, violet, purple. It reaches 8" – 16" (20 cm – 40 cm) high. 'Fairy Mix' is what I've had in my garden for years. It's great and has all of these hues.

# Lavatera trimestris
## 'Mont Blanc'

FAMILY NAME: *Malvaceae*
PHOTOGRAPHED IN THE GARDENS OF: Paddy Wales and Audrey Litherland

The sheer size and weight of this mallow makes it indispensable. I had no idea what it would be like when I was given some seeds many years ago. When it appeared in July of that year, I was overwhelmed by its beauty. The large white trumpet blossoms over sturdy but lithe stems fit right in among a host of perennials. And it has an almost aristocratic presence, it is so grand.

It is native to California, Australia, Canary Islands, the Mediterranean and the northwest Himalayas. The annual species, *L. trimestris*, is a Mediterranean native. I've seen huge plants almost like shrubs with pink flowers growing wild in the south of France. The blossoms are smaller but they have the same hairy stems and alternate and somewhat maple-shaped leaves. The flowers look a bit like hibiscus and come in pink, purply pink, lavender, red and white. They have five fluted petals. Behind each bloom there are three, six or nine bracts that form an involucre (collar), which distinguishes lavateras from true mallows (malvas), which have three bracts. These mallows are 3' – 5' (1 m – 1.5 m) high and grow like a small, well-proportioned shrub. But—and here's a great virtue— it is self-supporting and blooms from July right up to frost.

'Mont Blanc' happens to be my favorite cultivar because the white is so brilliant and refreshingly pure. The size, 2 feet (60 cm), is ideal for the proportions of the perennials I like to put it with. It's sturdy enough in form to

### PLANTING & MAINTENANCE TIPS

❦ This mallow takes just about any soil as long as it's well drained. It stands up to very hot sun but doesn't like getting moved about.

❦ Sow seeds after last frost where you want the plant to grow. Germination takes from 15 to 20 days. Or start flowers in peat pots a month before the last frost and put in place once the soil has warmed up sufficiently.

hold its own with *Euphorbia myrsinites*, which has almost waxy gray foliage, and *Dianthus* 'Mrs. Sinkins' with its steely gray foliage and bright white flowers.

Lavateras can be placed anywhere in a sunny border. They look quite wonderful with hollyhocks and around the bare nakedness of the lower parts of deep pink and white roses. This is another plant that goes really well with *Physostegia*, obedient plant, and the perennial giant lobelia. All three are in scale with each other. This is important when you are placing an annual with as much character as lavatera. Photographer Paddy Wales loves them as cut flowers. When placed in a china vase, they look as though they are made of china as well.

*Lavatera trimestris*
'Silver Cup'

*Lavatera trimestris* 'Mont Blanc'

## OTHER SPECIES & CULTIVARS

*L. trimestris* 'Silver Cup' is rose-pink with a bloom 3" – 4" (7.5 cm – 10 cm) across; grows to 2 feet (60 cm). 'Loveliness' has deep rose-pink blooms; grows to 20 inches (50 cm). 'Mont Rose' is smaller than 'Silver Cup'. 'Pink Beauty' is pale pink; 2 feet (60 cm) high; var. *alba* has white blooms.

*L. arborea*, tree mallow, grows 3' – 10' (1 m – 3 m) with thick erect stems. Stemless flowers. 'Variegata' has variegated dark and light with cream foliage. Must be propagated by cuttings; won't come true from seed.

# *Lobelia erinus* 'Crystal Palace'

FAMILY NAME: *Lobeliaceae*

PHOTOGRAPHED IN THE GARDEN OF: Barbara Mason

L obelias are just about the best carpet plant of all the annuals. There is an intensity to this plant that makes it a very good background for less showy plants or ones that might fade in midsummer. And it's jaunty enough to perk up any part of the garden it's put in. This fine old plant is native to South Africa, where it's a perennial. There are from 200 to 365 species. In North America it's one of our most familiar annuals, valued for

*Lobelia erinus* 'Crystal Palace'

❧ Must have cool, moist, rich soil and doesn't like being dried out. Amend with leaf mold if possible. In the north it can take sun, but in warmer areas it will thrive best in light shade.

❧ The seed is very fine; cover to germinate; indoors, start at least 10 weeks before the last frost. Set out 6 inches (15 cm) apart.

❧ Cut back in midsummer or when they start looking a bit ratty. They will bloom again right until frost kills them off.

its compact form and tremendously long period of bloom.

The tiny, very intense blossoms almost cover up the green-purple leaves. There are now forms in red, light blue, pink, violet and white. The cobalt blue of *L. erinus* 'Crystal Palace' makes a spectacular swath as a carpet plant around perennials, and it's easy to shear back once the first blooming period is over. I have it in a semi-shady border where it runs around all sorts of other plants such as ornamental grasses, creeping thymes and other perennials with bright, bright flowers such as *Saponaria ocymoides*, soapwort. Another good combination is with *Heuchera micrantha* 'Palace Purple', whose pale blossoms float above the denseness of the purple foliage in both plants.

Lobelias are traditional edging plants because they can fill in almost any niche provided for them in a most cheerful way. The trailing forms are ideal for floating over the edges of pots. 'Blue Cascade' has light blue flowers; 'Red Cascade' purple-red flowers with a white eye; 'Sapphire', bright blue with white eye, is one of the most commonly available.

## OTHER SPECIES & CULTIVARS

*L. erinus* has many varieties, and these are just a few more:

'Blue Moon', larger blooms and cobalt blue, 4 inches (10 cm); 'Cambridge Blue', clear sky blue, grows to 4 inches (10 cm); 'Queen Victoria', cardinal red; 'Rosamund', cherry red with a white eye, 6 inches (15 cm); 'White Lady', white flowers.

*L. cardinalis* is the familiar brilliantly colored cardinal flower, a perennial with toothed leaves that blooms between July and October. Native from New Brunswick to Florida to Texas, this is a woodland wildflower in its native habitat. 'Alba' is the white form; 'Rosea' the pink.

*L. siphilitica*, the perennial lobelia, is a terrific plant with spiky deep blue flowers. It does best in semi-shade. 'Blue & White', clear blue and white; needs moist soil. Self-seeds; grows to 3 feet (1 m).

# *Matthiola incana*

FAMILY NAME: *Cruciferae*
PHOTOGRAPHED IN: the VanDusen Botanical Garden

This is the plant to make the garden a scented idyll at night. Though they are fragrant during the day, at night they exude an even more magnificent bouquet. This is a hardy annual to have close to a deck or seating area. There are three series in this genus:

*Brompton Series*, biennials, good scent, and a huge color range. Sow seeds in summer, plant out in fall; grows to 18 inches (45 cm).

*Park Series*, those sown in early spring for autumn are treated as annuals; those sown in autumn for spring are treated as biennials—the grayish green foliage will appear the first year, the flowers the year after; grows to 1 foot (30 cm); scented four-petalled flowers.

*Ten-week Series* are the most frequently grown and that's how long it takes them to bloom. Shrubby, self-supporting 1 foot (30 cm) tall plants.

Stocks grow 1' – 3' (30 cm – 1 m), depending on the cultivar. There are

*Matthiola incana*

❧ An easy-to-grow, cold-resistant annual that will crumple during extremely high temperatures. It usually takes full sun but will tolerate some shade in rich, well-drained soil. Add organic matter and lime.

❧ Make successive sowings of stocks: they will bloom in June and July from March sowings; in August and September from May sowings. Germination takes 14 days at 80°F/26°C. They don't transplant well.

❧ Don't let seedlings dry out. Plant 1 foot (30 cm) apart in late April; for later blooms sow directly in the garden barely covered with soil.

❧ In mild regions, sow seeds in place in the autumn.

❧ For double forms, leave the palest seedling in place and trash the rest.

50 species in the genus, which includes annuals, biennials and perennials. In its native Mediterranean, this is a subshrub. There are only two species in cultivation.

*M. incana*, stock or gillyflower, has dozens of cultivars; grows 1' – 2½' (30 cm – 75 cm) high with 1 inch (2.5 cm) wide usually double blooms in white, blue, purple, pink and yellowish. An old-fashioned plant that provides good late color in the garden. This is a somewhat bushy upright plant.

I usually scatter the seeds among other plants and watch what they do. This is an important plant to have near the house to appreciate the

magnificent scent at night. I put them with *Hesperis matronalis*, dame's rocket, another self-seeder that also has a similar demeanor and marvellous presence. It comes in white, lilac and purple.

Use these plants in containers, for the cutting bed, or just about anywhere. Plant the single-flowered varieties where it won't bother you or other plants if they seed themselves all over. One friend has Cos lettuce in her garden and swears that they do much better in the shade of stocks. She has them hedged in with *Buxus*, box, in one area. The effect is striking.

### OTHER SPECIES & CULTIVARS

*M. bicornis*, night scented stock, is a subspecies of *M. longipetala*. Though the lilac flowers look like nothing much during the day, in the late evening they open up and release their fragrance. Grows to 1 foot (30 cm).

*M. longipetala*, evening stock, hardy annual, not a spectacular plant, with white to purple flowers that open up as the light fades; 1' – 2' (30 cm – 60 cm); branches about halfway up the grayish foliage. Plant anywhere after last frost; flowers two months after sowing; will self-seed.

*Matthiola incana*

# *Nemophila maculata*

FAMILY NAME: *Hydrophyllaceae*
PHOTOGRAPHED IN: the Park & Tilford Gardens

*Nemophila maculata*

Whenever a tiny spot in the garden opens up, consider five-spot as a filler. Here is a splendid annual that takes some shade. They are cool-weather wildflowers in their native sites, and anyone living in northern high altitudes will appreciate these pretty little plants.

There are from 11 to 18 species and about 50 forms and varieties. All are native to the United States, and you'll find them in the wild in California, Texas and Arkansas. They can be used in exactly the same way you use impatiens since both can accommodate sun or shade and like to flop about in a graceful manner.

*Nemophila maculata*, five-spot, is a hardy annual that differs from the

❧ Nemophilas cannot take searing sun—they will wither and fade. Any nemophilas grown in some sun, though, will be smaller, more compact and very floriferous. In the shade they'll bloom much longer. They prefer moderately fertile soil with plenty of organic matter. If you can't provide this, spread lots of compost or manure on the soil. Sow seeds as soon as the ground can be worked in a protected site where they can flower in early spring; they don't take well to transplanting. Germination takes two weeks, and plants should flower seven to eight weeks after sowing.

❧ Deadhead for a second flush of blooms.

❧ Keep weeds at bay with regular cultivation.

❧ Watch for aphids, and hit the plant regularly with a stream of water from the hose to keep them clean.

other popular species, *N. menziesii*, baby-blue-eyes, in a technical aspect that has to do with the seeds. This form is dwarf. Though this is a mainly prostrate plant, growing only to 6 inches (15 cm), it has hairy stems that branch out 1 foot (30 cm) in all directions. The thick, hairy flower stalks are 1" – 2" (2.5 cm – 5 cm) long; the leaves are opposite and mostly oblong and lobed. The small erect flowers are bell-shaped, white with dark purple at the tips of each petal, 2 inches (5 cm) across.

var. *albida* is white.

var. *grandiflora* is the larger form.

var. *purpurea* is marbled blue.

All forms lend themselves to hanging baskets. *N. m.* '5 Spot' grows to 6 inches (15 cm) and stems trail for 1 foot (30 cm); pale blue with deep blue veins. Ideal for a shady spot under a pergola or in front of a window on the veranda.

What a terrific edger this plant is if it's placed about a foot (30 cm) from the edge so it can lean forward. This will soften hard stone patios and steps or mark the beginning of a woodland garden. It's a good plant as an annual ground cover and simple to grow from seed. Plant it with herbs. Grow it in pots that can be combined with other trailing plants such as lobelias.

This plant looks dramatic under the protection and shade of such other strong gray plants as lavenders and helichrysums. One hortbuddy has a washbasin filled with water to reflect the nemophilas planted all around it.

*Nemophila maculata*

## OTHER SPECIES & CULTIVARS

*N. menziesii*, baby-blue-eyes, is a hardy annual from California that grows to 1 foot (30 cm). The bell-shaped bright blue flowers with white centres top bright green serrated foliage. It is dense, spreading but also erect. Ideal for naturalizing. Blooms from June to September.

'Pennie Black' grows 2" – 4" (5 cm – 10 cm) and trails 12" – 15" (30 cm – 38 cm); flowers have almost purple to black centres with a silvery white scalloped edge. Good plant for edging.

# *Nicotiana sylvestris*

FAMILY NAME: *Solanaceae*
PHOTOGRAPHED IN: Stanley Park

A nnuals that take a little shade are among our most useful plants. The flowering tobacco is one of them. The hotter the area, the more it favors a site that has protection from the afternoon sun.

The foliage on these plants is not the most beautiful, but the flowers, especially those with the most scent, are spectacular. Hummingbirds favor them. I put nicotianas wherever there is some shade but especially next to an *Aconitum*, monkshood, that grows near the deck at the back of the house.

There are 70 species in the genus *Nicotiana*, mostly tropical, all from the Americas, except for one found in Australia. They flower nonstop from June to first frost. In warm zones such as 9 and 10 they are perennial, but

*Nicotiana sylvestris*

otherwise they are desirable annuals. Tender annuals at that.

The basal rosettes can be as much as 1' – 2' (30 cm – 60 cm) across. But it's the large pendant trumpets that flute upward into almost a star-like configuration that are the main attraction. Flowers cluster at the end of branches. The great big soft leaves are alternate. One caveat with this plant—all parts are poisonous, so be careful about placing it where children might play.

*N. tabacum* is the tabacco plant that has been traded and smoked for centuries. It may grow to 8 feet (2.5 m) and is seldom grown in gardens.

Most nicotianas can tolerate frost and do much better with cooler rather than hot, humid weather. They like sun but can accept some shade.

*N. sylvestris* (similar to *N. alata*), a huge plant 5' – 6' (1.5 m – 2 m), is a native of Argentina. The sheer size makes it an iffy choice for a very small garden. But two or three create a stunning corner arrangement in a raised bed—making them appear even more statuesque than they already are. The long white tubular flowers look almost like giant lilies. They remain open during the day, and at night they give off scent that attracts moths. This one will bloom well in a light shade. There are enormous basal rosettes of paddle-like leaves.

This is one of the favorite forms of English garden writer Rosemary Verey. She plants them in pots to bring indoors for the evening. The fragrance will waft through the whole house. In this variety the brown seedpods are

## PLANTING & MAINTENANCE TIPS

❧ Best to plant in sun with some shade in the afternoon if the area is hot. Thrives in soil rich with organic matter. Pinch back to stimulate branching and water during dry spells.

❧ Nicotine hybrids will self-seed but they won't come true to parents. Keep deadheaded to avoid this problem.

❧ It takes about eight weeks from germination to flowers. Start indoors in daytime temperatures from 50 to 55°F (10 to 13°C). They need light to germinate, which takes two to three weeks. In late March, scatter seeds over soil in flats; keep in a sunny spot for one month. Transplant to richer growing medium and start lowering temperatures. Water from below (set flats in large flat pans with pebbles on the bottom). After two to three weeks of lowered temperatures, put outdoors in a cold frame to harden off for transplanting in May. This is a dense plant, so space 1' – 1½' (30 cm – 45 cm) apart.

❧ Pests: for whitefly, spray directly with soapy water; for slugs, handpick.

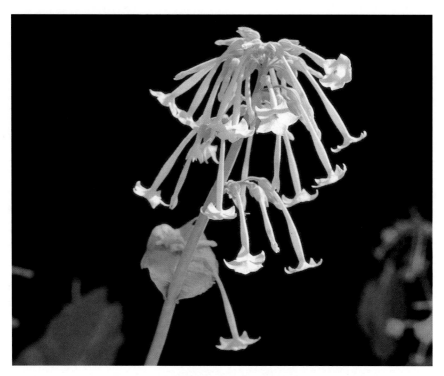

*Nicotiana sylvestris*

decorative enough to be added to dried flower arrangements. Collect seeds on a dry day in autumn. I try to put them with different plants each year, but they do look wonderful with almost any of the silver-foliage artemisias or *Stachys*, lamb's-ears; *Cynara cardunculus,* cardoon; and *Centaurea cyanus,* bachelor's-buttons; both with gray foliage and bright blue flowers.

## OTHER SPECIES & CULTIVARS

*N. alata (N. affinis),* half-hardy annual, are the most familiar of all the hybrids. Commonly called jasmine tabacco. The 'Domino' series of cultivars grow to 1 foot (30 cm). Compact plants with 2 inches (5 cm) flowers at the end of each stem: ruby red, deep rose, lime green and white.

'Grandiflora'; by August candelabras rise to 5 feet (1.5 m), the framework invisible in the night; fragrant.

'Nicki' series, at 20 inches (50 cm) tall, are rather more bushy plants with stems branching at ground level.

'Sensation' grows to 4 feet (1.2 m).

Scented species: *N. longiflora, N. suaveolens, N. sylvestris.*

# Nigella damascena

FAMILY NAME: *Ranunculaceae*
PHOTOGRAPHED IN THE GARDEN OF: Peter and Patricia Wright

Gertrude Jekyll, the great English landscape gardener, used this wonderful old-fashioned annual in her designs not only for the color of the blooms but even more so for the fine lacy foliage and conspicuous highly ornamental seedpods, which stand erect in a sprightly manner.

A native of the Mediterranean, nigellas have been in cultivation for well over 400 years. There are at least 12 species in the genus. They have long tap roots, which does not make them easy candidates to move around once you've got them in place. The many-branched erect stems have almost lacy foliage with a solitary flower at the end.

*Nigella damascena*

❧ Ordinary soil is good enough for these plants as long as it is well drained. Open sunny locations are the favorite venue.

❧ They grow easily from seed: barely cover seeds with soil. Flowers appear in eight to ten weeks.

❧ Flowering starts in early summer, and slightly earlier from fall sowings. Use coarse, porous fertile soil for pots. Don't let them get overly wet—this will cause rotting.

❧ Deadhead to keep plants producing blooms.

❧ Self-sows, but the blooms get smaller and smaller each year.

We think of nigellas as blue, but there are now white and pale pink forms. They have five petals with a collar of very fine bracts. When this plant is in the ideal site, it will naturalize harmoniously almost anywhere in the garden. Once the bloom has passed, pale green seedpods with burnt sienna markings develop.

*N. damascena*, love-in-a-mist, blooms in summer in pale rose, pink and deep blue or a slightly off white. Grows to $1\frac{1}{2}'$ – 2' (45 cm – 60 cm). 'Miss Jekyll', semi-double blue or white blooms; epithets such as "diaphanous" and "gossamer" come instantly to mind when thinking about the feathery quality of the foliage. 'Persian Jewels' is a mixture of blue, pink, white, carmine, mauve and violet flowers. They make good long-lasting cut flowers. Cut when the burgundy stripes begin to appear on the puffy balloon-like pods. Then hang upside down and allow to dry out for flower arrangements. Combine with any of the gray-foliage plants, especially artemesias. Mass them, or allow to form drifts if you have enough space. Combine with blue delphiniums, blue lupins and peonies.

## OTHER SPECIES & CULTIVARS

*N. hispanica* is a coarser plant with small seedpods and more linear rather than thread-like leaves.

*N. sativa* is fernlike but less finely divided than *N. damascena*; pale blue flowers; edible seed called Roman coriander or black cumin. Sprouting takes two weeks. Space 8 inches (20 cm) apart; doesn't transplant easily.

# *Papaver rhoeas*

FAMILY NAME: *Papaveraceae*
PHOTOGRAPHED IN THE GARDEN OF: Pam Frost

Poppies are one of the most traditional of all the annuals. They are easy to grow and will naturalize in large groups. Their nodding heads dancing in the breeze seem to be crucial to the sense of well-being on a blithe summer day. They even attract bees. There are 100 species in the genus, found mainly in the Mediterranean region, though some come from Asia and one is found in South Africa and in Australia. The seeds, flowers and sap have long been used for both good and evil purposes. Poppies have long been associated with sleep and death.

Because the color range of the 2 inch (5 cm) flowers is so vast—apricot, orange, yellow, cream, pink, rose, purple, red, white, bicolored—there is a poppy that can be useful with almost any other annuals and perennials. The colors are pure, the texture of the petals like gossamer. Then there are the pistils, which turn into impressive seedpods once the flowers have gone.

Most poppies bloom at the end of a slender wiry stalk 8" – 10" (20 cm – 25 cm). The flat buds open up with a faint scent, usually one flower with four petals for each stem. The crinkly-edged leaves grow from a rosette at the base. Though poppies don't last very long—only a few days—the trick here is to make successive sowings so that they keep coming along for weeks and weeks. Many of them self-sow like mad all over the place, so you have to be careful about how many you want, and their function.

*P. rhoeas*, corn poppy, is the traditional Flanders fields poppy. It produces edible seeds. This is a hardy annual native to Europe and Asia that grows on 2' – 3' (60 cm – 1 m) stems. The flowers open into a brilliant red with silky, opaque unequal petals—two large and two small. The wiry stems branch out and the foliage is dark green. Seeds sown in the ground in early spring will bloom 60 days later. Remove seedpods and the bloom will be continuous.

Shirley poppies, a strain of *P. rhoeas*, come in white, pink, rose, salmon and bicolor and in singles and doubles. 'Mother of Pearl' is called fairy wings and grows 10" – 14" (25 cm – 35 cm). 'Shirley Re-selected Double Mixed' grows 2 feet (60 cm). The narrow or lance-shaped divided leaves are dark green. The willowy silk-downed stems carry enchanting ruffled flowers. The seed capsules have a gray cast, the leaves are a dark green. More cultivars are produced each year and there are more than 30 named forms and varieties in this species alone. The appellation Shirley came because an English vicar, Rev. W. Wilks, started selecting out unusual seeds at the vicarage garden at Shirley. He chose ones that were whiter and paler with each generation, changing the black centres to yellow.

*P. somniferum*, opium poppies, are the source of both codeine and opium. In some places in North America it is illegal to grow this species. These imposing plants have a noble demeanor. They have magnificent gray-blue fringed leaves. The huge seedpods can be dried for use in flower arrangements. This is a hardy annual native to Europe and western Asia. It has incredible 4 inch (10 cm) white, pink, rose and purple blooms that look like great big folded handkerchiefs.

'Danebrog' has fringed petals. 'Peony Flowered Pink Beauty' has double blossoms in salmon pink; 'P. F. Mixed' grows 2' – 3' (60 cm – 1 m) and has 4 inch (10 cm) double blooms with gray-green foliage. 'White Cloud' has extra-double large white flowers; 'Alba' is white. 'Hens & Chickens', 2' – 2½' (30 cm – 75 cm) has particularly large decorative seedheads.

All poppies look wonderful massed in an almost meadow-like situation; in fact, they are amazing flowers to let naturalize in a poor, dry site. I've seen whole hillsides in the south of France brilliant with the watermelon pink of a native poppy. The more dwarf species are good for the rock garden.

Poppies are the one plant I don't mind dotted about. Grow with other plants in such a way that holes won't be left once they've finished blooming. For instance, the low-growing, 2 inch (5 cm) *Portulaca umbraticola* looks wonderful with the cheeky colors of Shirley poppies, and the gray foliage looks good together. Poppies make excellent cut flowers when taken just as the bud is about to open; plunge the end immediately into very

*Papaver rhoeas*

❧ All poppies do their best in full sun. This is a plant with long tap roots, so it doesn't transplant easily, therefore any seeds started indoors should be sown in peat pots to be set in place in spring. Apart from that, it's easy to grow in almost any kind of soil, though they prefer poor, dry soils (given where they come from, this is understandable).

❧ Plant seeds directly in the garden in spring or sow in fall sprinkled in with other hardy annuals or bulbs such as tulips.

❧ Poppy seeds are so fine they should be mixed with double the amount of sand before sowing and scattered very thinly in place. Top with a light layer of soil and make sure it doesn't dry out.

❧ After germination, thin *P. rhoeas* and hybrids 8" – 10" (20 cm – 25 cm) apart. (It doesn't have a long bloom period, so seeds should be sown every two weeks in spring. Don't overwater. This poppy fades in very high temperatures.)

❧ Keep deadheading. And make successive sowings a few weeks apart until midsummer. This way there will be blooms all summer long.

❧ Annual poppies naturalize by self-seeding.

hot water, or sear it with a match, before putting in a vase.

Here's a combination with poppies that one of the finest gardeners in the country has in her high front border: amber alstroemerias, pink lavateras, blue anchusas, daisies and yellow roses. Other plants to put with poppies: nicotianas, verbenas and asters, underplanted with violas and Viper's Bugloss.

## OTHER SPECIES & CULTIVARS

*P. burseri* (*P. alpinum*), native to the mountains of Europe; compact gray short basal rosettes; 4" – 5" (10 cm – 12.5 cm); white to gold flowers grow to 8 inches (20 cm). Blooms quickly from seed. Treat as a biennial rather than a perennial. Zone 5.

*P. nudicaule*, Iceland poppies, are native to Arctic regions. They are evergreen hardy, perennials (treated as biennials); flowers are pink, white, salmon and red; blooms longer than other poppies. Stems are 15 inches (38 cm) tall. Needs well-drained soil; can't take too much moisture. 'Garden Gnome Mixed' is very hardy. Zones 2 to 9.

*P. orientale*, oriental poppy, is a long-lived perennial that does not like being disturbed. Can be propagated by division. 'Dwarf Allegro' grows 16" – 20" (40 cm – 50 cm).

## CALIFORNIA BLUEBELL

# *Phacelia campanularia*

FAMILY NAME: *Hydrophyllaceae*
PHOTOGRAPHED IN THE GARDEN OF: Glen Patterson

What a superb plant this is. Phacelias love hot weather. The spritely comportment of this hardy annual is addictive and not just to bees.
There are 114 to 175 species in this genus of herbaceous perennials and annuals native to the southwest U.S. (the Mojave desert of southern California) and Mexico. Annual species and varieties are the most widely used. They have simple or compound alternate leaves, sometimes with hairy veins prominent on the underside, slightly fuzzy, reddish when young. The 1 inch (2.5 cm) flowers have short stalks and five petals; the centres contain yellow pollen attractive to insects.

*Phacelia campanularia*

The vivid blue is one reason why this is a popular annual. Very good as container plants, phacelias can also be allowed to interweave with other plants in a low border.

*P. campanularia*, California bluebell, has upturned 1 inch (2.5 cm) wide gentian blue flowers with white anthers; blooms between July and September; grows to 9 inches (22 cm). If they are crushed, however, the scented leaves can cause dermatitis in some people. The gray-green foliage has a slight red tinge that can barely be seen because the plant has so many blooms.

Plant these seeds along with California poppies. They both have the same cultural needs, and the phacelias will take over when the poppies have gone. Phacelias are also tremendous annuals with astilbes.

In containers, bluebells make a flashy show. They tumble over the edges and are striking with white impatiens. Anyone with the deep-seated need to have orange in the garden should consider putting orange flowers with a blue of this intensity—the two colors have an affinity for each other. It's possible to fill a pot with phacelias and *Calendula*, pot marigold, for a great contrast between stiff and supple foliage and these two intense hues.

## PLANTING & MAINTENANCE TIPS

❧ A sun-loving annual not fussy about what soil it's planted in. These are desert plants, however, so sandy, well-drained soil is the most suitable. The small seeds need no cover, but they don't transplant well. Broadcast seed and rake lightly; when seedlings are 1¾ inches (3 cm), thin to 7 inches (18 cm). Flowers in seven to eight weeks. In zones 3 to 8, sow seeds outdoors after last frost. In zones 9 and 10, sow seeds in autumn for spring blooming.

❧ Water as much as possible during very hot weather.

❧ Shear back after blooming for a second lot of flowers.

❧ Don't let this one self-seed; they tend to come back in wimpy colors.

## OTHER SPECIES & CULTIVARS

*P. congesta*, lavender flowers, grows to 2 feet (60 cm).

*P. dubia* 'Lavender Lass' grows to 1 foot (30 cm). Soft blue and white blooms, suitable for sun or shade.

*P. parryi* 'Royal Admiral' is a new introduction. Even more intense than other phacelia blues. Grows 1' – 1½' (30 cm – 45 cm) high. Hardy annual.

# *Salvia farinacea*

FAMILY NAME: *Labiatae*
PHOTOGRAPHED IN: West Vancouver Memorial Park

*Salvia farinacea*

Finding glorious spiky forms in the midsummer garden is a wonderful experience. These relatives of the sage we use in cooking are amiable plants that work almost anywhere in the garden. For those who are developing xeriscape gardens—ones where the design is dependent on using drought-tolerant plants—salvias will solve many problems.

Like all members of this family, *S. farinacea*, blue salvia, mealycup sage, has square stems. Its silver, slender heart-shaped leaves make a good separator for brightly colored flowers. Violet-blue flower spikes grow 2' – 3' (60 cm – 90 cm) high. This tender perennial is usually grown as a half-hardy annual; it's a native of New Mexico and Texas. And it's a good dried flower

❧ The only absolutely ironclad rule about salvias is to put them in the sun—they hate shade. But there are few other problems connected with the plant. Any well-drained soil will do. I always use plants that have been started in the nursery. If you do start them indoors, the seeds must be kept warm and have light to germinate. Space them 1 foot (30 cm) apart. Or sow them in place once it warms up—but it takes ages for them to flower.

❧ *S. farinacea* has large seeds that germinate fairly quickly.

as well. This aromatic herb is attractive to bees.

'Victoria' takes fourteen weeks to produce rich violet-blue spikes. A good cutting flower, this hybrid is considered choice. Grows to 1½ feet (45 cm). 'Blue Bedder' has Wedgwood blue flowers; grows to 2 feet (60 cm).

One of the very best salvias of all is *S. viridis* (*S. Horminium*), clary sage; it has spikes at the end of stems that go to 1½ feet (45 cm) high. 'Claryssa', 1½ feet (45 cm) is a new dwarf strain, more compact, brighter colors; 'Claryssa Blue', 'Claryssa Pink' and 'Claryssa White'. It combines so well with almost anything in the garden—the glorious grays of *Artemisia stelleriana, Centaurea cyanus,* bachelor's-buttons, and annual larkspur. I have an *Achillea* 'White Thaler', which is a very clear white, and the silver and blue of this salvia mixes in fantastically well with it. Put it with such strong plants as *Hesperis matronalis, Coreopsis verticillata* 'Moonbeam' and *Sedum* 'Autumn Joy'; *Lysimachia clethroides,* campanulas and tradescantia. I also have it with an ornamental grass, *Helictotrichon,* which has steel blue blades; these wonderful spikes look great poking above them.

## OTHER SPECIES & CULTIVARS

*S. coccinea,* red salvia, scarlet blooms with black stems; grows to 3 feet (90 cm).

'Cherry Blossom', 12" – 15" (30 cm – 38 cm); 'Lady in Red', warm red bedding plant good for containers.

*S. splendens,* an exotic from Brazil; tender annual that grows up to 3 feet (90 cm) in the most vibrant, brilliant red. This is a major prejudice on my part, but there are few places I can imagine this plant except in a garden designed for a riot of color. Maybe in a container to perk up a dull corner. Dwarf cultivars bloom from late May or early June, taller ones from early June. 'Blaze of Fire' is smaller, 1 foot (30 cm), and stays neat.

## NASTURTIUM

# *Tropaeolum majus*

FAMILY NAME: *Tropaeolaceae*
PHOTOGRAPHED IN THE GARDEN OF: Pam Frost

E verywhere in the summer garden the great lily-pad leaves of *Tropaeolum*, nasturtiums, make my heart leap. There is something extraordinary about these low plants that will cheerfully attract pests such as aphids to their charming flowers. And if you have a garden that can't accommodate orange, there are now such glorious cultivars that it's possible to have a whole palette of nasturtiums. A friend once pointed out that I must have very poor soil to be able to grow so many nasturtiums. That certainly startled me. I suppose I'd heard that nasturtiums prefer poor soil but ignored the caveat. My garden supports hundreds of other plants in tandem, and none of them seem to suffer. Perhaps I might be equally astonished at how much better my nasturtiums would do if I did have poor soil.

Native to South Africa, they are wildflowers in tropical countries of the new world from Mexico to Chile and throughout the Andes. There is no

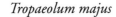

*Tropaeolum majus*

other plant as popular and easy to grow from seed—it's an experience I wouldn't want to miss each year.

All the hybrids sold commercially come from either *T. majus* or *T. minus*. I steered clear of them for years because what was available at the local garden centre was a mix of colors—not enough control for me. Then I discovered the ones from a specialty catalogue (see the Bibliography for specialty seed houses) and now look for new colors each year.

There are few functions that nasturtiums can't fill. It is a good cut flower, it's edible, and it looks superb in hanging baskets and containers. There are single and double as well as climbing forms. They seldom exceed 1 foot (30 cm), and the climbers can get as high as 10 feet (3 m). The 2 inch (5 cm) flowers have spurs, a slight sharp scent and an enormous color range; there's the traditional orange, yellow and red along with salmon, salmon pink, deep pink, cherry, ecru and crimson. The double-flowered varieties have stronger scent.

I mentioned the leaves were like lily pads, and they do have that pale green watery quality to them. They can also be eaten. Some people pickle the seedpods just the way they do capers. As though all these virtues weren't enough, these are a trap plant without equal. They draw aphids away from other plants, which makes them valuable in vegetable patches.

Where I live there are areas with entire front gardens given over to nasturtiums, usually in the bright mixes you buy in grocery stores. The effect is dazzling. The vine forms crawl up ugly telephone poles, making them objects of beauty.

*T. majus* is a semi-trailing, scented hardy annual, 1 foot (30 cm) high. 'Double Gleam Mixed' is a semi-double in yellow, orange and scarlet.

The most useful for containers and small gardens are the *T. nanum* hybrids: I've always had great luck with the 'Whirlybird' series. I usually get cream or scarlet and use the former with pale astilbes and the latter in a Japanese pot that's the color of an old-fashioned ginger jar.

'Alaska Mixed', 8 inches (20 cm) tall, is a dwarf semi-double variety that has variegated foliage. The mix includes cherry rose, gold, mahogany, orange, scarlet, tangerine and cream, with not a faulty tone in the lot. There's also 'Empress of India' with a crimson flower; it's worth trying because of the dark foliage.

Nasturtiums look good with daylilies, which come in almost as many colors and lots of them in the same hue. One of my favorite English garden writers, Christopher Lloyd, uses 'Golden Gleam' with *Anemone japonica*, Japanese anemone, whose yellow centres pick out the color of the nasturtiums. I put them with the steely blue-stemmed forms of dianthus, a huge old daisy and *Alchemilla mollis*, which has its own velvety sage green leaves.

In tubs they should drip over the sides. Or let them clamber over a south-facing fence for a dramatic look. At the edges of raised beds they add a cheerful glow.

Paddy Wales observes wisely that nasturtiums are one of those edible flowers that, when put in a salad, are carefully picked out. But they look good, and I like the peppery taste they add. She has found that in a breezy spot they won't get black aphids, and that fertilizer seems to slow them down because they put too much effort into leaves; stress and poor soil keep them in bloom.

There is a south-facing garden in her neighborhood with a deck edged by four large cedar planters each jammed with different-colored nasturtiums: pale yellow, amber, bright orange and bronze all trailing over the edge. This is certainly a lighthearted effort with only the occasional watering to be concerned about.

## PLANTING & MAINTENANCE TIPS

❧ Ordinary soil is fine, but the best is a light, sandy medium. These guys thrive on being deprived. There must be good drainage, since they can't take too much water—it encourages leaf development at the expense of flowers.

❧ Not easy to transplant, but can be sown outdoors before the first frost. Cover with soil to a depth three times the width of the seed.

❧ Plant dwarf varieties 7 inches (18 cm) apart.

❧ Aphids are attracted to nasturtiums. Either view it as a trap plant and pick the blooms off by hand, or wait for the aphids to attract ladybugs, who will do the job for you.

❧ Said to repel squash bugs and some beetles.

## OTHER SPECIES & CULTIVARS

*T. majus* 'Peach Melba' has light yellow blooms with a red blotch at the throat.

*T. minus* forms a dwarf bush about 1 foot (30 cm) high to make a good edging or ground cover.

*T. nanum*, flame flower, another climber, 6' – 10' (2 m – 3 m), considered difficult; scarlet blooms.

'Alaska Mixed' has variegated cream and green leaves; grows 6' – 10' (2 m – 3 m) and blooms all summer. This twining variety can make its way along a fence or hedge and looks quite beautiful mixed up with ivy as a screening plant.

*T. peregrinum*, canary bird vine, has five-lobed leaves and small brilliant yellow flowers with feathery petals.

# *Verbena bonariensis*

FAMILY NAME: *Verbenaceae*
PHOTOGRAPHED IN THE GARDEN OF: Mr. & Mrs. W. L. Sauders

Its spectacular height and statuesque quality make *Verbena bonariensis* a terrific plant for the late-summer garden. It stands erect without staking. The purple flowers add to the rich tones that precede autumn's great flush. And they are around for a long time.

Verbenas belong to a huge family (anywhere from 2,000 to 3,000

*Verbena bonariensis* with *Cleome spinosa*

❧ Plant in the sun. Verbenas don't do well in the shade at all. If you live in a very hot, dry area, some shade from the afternoon sun is preferable. Grow in well-drained light soil with organic matter added.

❧ Seeds are difficult to germinate, and it's wiser to try indoor seeding rather than directly in the soil. Chill seeds in the fridge for a week, then plant in pots; leave them in a dark place for three weeks. Then transplant into the garden once there is no danger of frost—about the same time as you put out tomato plants. Space 8" – 12" (20 cm – 30 cm) apart.

❧ For containers: use a medium of equal parts sand, peat and leaf mold.

❧ Cut back after the first flowering to produce more flowers in the following few weeks.

❧ Pests do attack this plant—slugs, aphids, whitefly and leaf miners. Hand-picking or hitting them with a hose or a dose of soapy water occasionally will help.

❧ Powdery mildew can affect some verbenas—make sure they have plenty of water in early summer and good air circulation around them.

members) in which there are 75 genera, and in this genus alone there are more than 200 species. Plants with the name *verbena* that don't belong in this genus are lemon verbena (*Aloysia triphylla*), sand verbena (*Abronia*) and sand-verbena myrtle (*Backhousia*).

All plants in this part of the family are treated as annuals or tender perennials. They are generally small, self-supporting plants with 2 inch (5 cm) flowers in clusters of 10 to 20 blossoms of blue, red, pink or deep purple with white centres or eyes. They bloom in midsummer and, given their size, 6" – 16" (15 cm – 40 cm), are ideal for both pot and rock garden, with *Dianthus* spp., sweet alyssum and silver-foliage plants. They come in all shapes and forms—spreading, trailing, prostrate—and every tint but yellow.

*V. bonariensis* is a native of South America introduced into gardens in 1732. It grows from 3' – 6' (1 m – 2 m), with a spread of 1 foot (30 cm). The branching, wiry, hairy stems come from basal clumps of toothed leaves. The tufts at the end of each stem are tiny purple-blue flowers that bloom in late summer. They come easily from seed. In fact, they not only self-seed but in hot spots they can bloom and seed themselves to death. Alas, never in my own garden. I have to do it every year.

This accommodating plant is unfortunately without any scent. It's a really good one to use over early blooming lilies. Given the loose formation, it also works well with shrub roses.

It must have space behind it to emphasize its inherent airiness. Or put it in a sunny area with a shady area behind. One of my favorite gardeners has *V. bonariensis* with gray-leaved and mauve-flowered plants—near *Buddleia*, butterfly bush, hardy geraniums, the magenta brilliance of *Lychnis coronaria*, and *Alchemilla mollis*, Lady's-mantle.

Interplant them with the strong grays of *Nepeta* spp., *Cineraria maritima*, *Ruta graveolens* and *Ballota*. They will disguise areas where poppies have disappeared and, combined with any of the larger asters such as *Aster* x *frikartii* 'Mönch', will make a splendid back of the border.

## OTHER SPECIES & CULTIVARS

*V. canadensis*, trailing verbena, is best in containers and hanging baskets. Native of North America. It's a 1' – 1½' (30 cm – 45 cm) hairy clump-forming plant. The multitude of branches grow along the ground with stems and flowers growing upwards. Purple-pink flowers bloom all summer into autumn.

*V.* x *hybrida*; the nice thing about this loose-jointed plant is that it will make new roots at nodes that touch the earth. The leaves are covered in hairs; flowers come in white, pink, red, lavender, blue and purple with a white or cream eye. This is a good plant in containers:

'Amethyst', cobalt blue; 'Armour Light Pink', pastel shades of soft pink and white; 'Blaze', scarlet; 'Blue Lagoon', true blue; 'Romance Lavender', 'Peaches and Cream'.

*V. peruviana*, Peruvian verbena, is good for a rock garden. Intense scarlet flowers carpet bright green foliage.

*V. rigida*, syn. *V. venosa*, vervain, perennial species, excellent grown from seed. Grows to 2 feet (60 cm); lavender-blue flowers from mid-summer onwards; dark green leaves borne on flower stems.

# *Viola cornuta* 'White Perfection'

FAMILY NAME: *Violaceae*
PHOTOGRAPHED IN THE GARDEN OF: Kathy Leishman

I love the anarchic nature of pansies. They are the free spirits of the garden, caring little about staying within the range of their own species. They will hybridize with any other pansy that grows nearby.

The funny faces of pansies make them, to some, the quintessential annual. The purple and yellow nodding heads have long been jammed into windowboxes or spread around gardens with quiet abandon. But given the work of the hybridizers, this plant has become much, much more. You can now find pansies in solid colors and pastels, blotched and bicolored.

Pansies were developed from *V. tricolor*, *V. lutea* and *V. altaica*, and the result is *V.* x *wittrockiana*. Annual pansies are frost hardy and grow 9 inches (22 cm) high with 2" – 5" (5 cm – 12.5 cm) wide flowers—one to a stem. They love the cool weather, but there are plenty of new heat-tolerant varieties that will flower all summer.

Depending on the cultivar, pansies can bloom from March to July

*Pansies*

when planted in spring, and from September to frost from fall planting (these ones will flower again in spring). They bloom even longer in the warmer regions. Small varieties overwinter best.

There is some confusion about just what a pansy is. It's in the same family as violas and violets, but the latter are smaller species and sold under those names. Pansies are half-hardy annuals, growing in soft clumps with simple basal leaves, sometimes lobed, often wrinkled. There are more than 400 named pansies, and growers tend to group them into two categories:
Grandifloras: large-flowered varieties such as 'Majestic Giant' and 'Super Majestic Giant'.
Multifloras: smaller-flowered varieties that bloom earlier.
Multifloras are probably the best choice for northern gardens since they are the toughest of a tough lot. Though they may have smaller blooms, there are usually more of them.

Pansies prefer cool weather, especially cool nights, which makes them ideal for coastal areas where they are so persistent they appear to be perennial.

*V. cornuta*, horned violet, tufted pansy, is a native of Spain and the parent of many cultivars. It has smaller flowers than x *wittrockiana*. This plant, with heart-shaped leaves, has flowers 1" – 1½" (2.5 cm – 4 cm) wide and grows 8 inches (20 cm) high. It blooms from March to Christmas in warm areas. This is a good little plant to knit disparate perennials together. Let it go and it will pop up unexpectedly everywhere. 'White Perfection', shown here, is the ultimate edging plant.

## PLANTING & MAINTENANCE TIPS

❧ Plant them where they are shielded from afternoon sun to prolong bloom, or give them light shade. Must have moist, well-drained soil with a little compost added.

❧ Keep pinching back to make them more compact and floriferous.

❧ Set out plants in early spring. Where winters do not drop below 20°F (–6°C), pansy seeds can be sown and mulched in fall for early spring bloom.

❧ For seeding *V. cornuta* or *V.* x *wittrockiana*: place seeds in fridge for several days before sowing. Sow in flats in a cool, dark place fairly early in the year—10 to 12 weeks before the last frost. Cover seeds with sand. They should sprout in a week. Water from the bottom and keep cool (65°F/18°C). Pot up after a month and move them outside when mean temperatures hit 40°F/5°C. Harden off in a cold frame and move into the garden when the soil can be worked.

*Viola cornuta* 'White Perfection'

Pansies can be planted with almost any vine, but are particularly adroit with clematis, which needs cool roots. Pansies are a much more captivating way to do this than placing a rock over them. Plant them in with cool-weather salad greens such as lettuce; in a raised urn with white cosmos like a sea all around; with astilbes, yarrows, veronicas and *Alchemilla mollis,* Lady's-mantle.

Tubs filled with pansies can be brought out all through the year for damage control. If something looks terrible or has gone to rack and ruin, let pansies take over. In light shade, pots of pansies will perk things up no end.

Pansies can be eaten, though I've used them only as decoration on a plate. I planted pansies of some sort years ago and they've self-seeded, changing each year—sometimes a smoky blue, other times a deep purple. It's another bit of serendipity that gardening dishes up on a regular basis.

## OTHER SPECIES & CULTIVARS

*V. tricolor,* Johnny-jump-up, heart's ease, is native to Europe; self-sows like crazy; 6" – 12" (15 cm – 30 cm) high; very small flowers ¾ inch (2 cm) across, purple, yellow and white; corolla is flattish and round, spreading stems; blooms May to September.

'Bowles Black' is an interesting black form with a yellow eye; 'Jolly Joker'.

*V. rafinesquii,* field pansy, grows to 1 foot (30 cm); ½ inch (1.5 cm) petals bluish-white to cream colored; leafy, often branched from base. Sow where it can be allowed to ramp about, and thin to 6 inches (15 cm) apart.

# Bibliography

Bennett, Jennifer, and Turid Forsyth. *The Harrowsmith Annual Garden.* Camden East, Ont.: Camden House, 1990.

Jones, Carolyn. *The Complete Guide to Bedding Plants for Amateurs and Experts.* Vancouver: Whitecap Books, 1990.

Loewer, Peter. *The Annual Garden.* Emmaus, Pa.: Rodale Press, 1988.

McGourty, Frederick. *Annuals, 1001 Gardening Questions Answered.* Pownal, Vt.: Storey Communications, 1989.

Marston, Ted, ed. *Annuals; compiled from the Good Housekeeping illustrated encyclopedia of gardening.* New York: Hearst Books, 1993.

*Taylor's Guide to Annuals.* New York: Chanticleer Press Inc., 1986.

## SEED CATALOGUES

Many of the annual varieties mentioned in this book are from the Thompson & Morgan Seed Catalogue. I've always found this catalogue useful, and they will send seeds—very quickly—anywhere in North America with just a phone call. The catalogue doesn't oversell in its blurbs, and the seeds have always done well for me. There are other specialty catalogues I couldn't do without. I count on them for searching out new varieties. Check your local area first to ensure the hardiest seeds possible. Then branch out using these interesting catalogues.

Thompson & Morgan Inc., P.O. Box 1308, Jackson, NJ 08527-0308

Gardenimport Inc., P.O. Box 760, Thornhill, ON L3T 4A5
(carries Sutton's Seeds Ltd. from England)

Dominion Seed House, 115 Guelph St., Georgetown, ON L7G 4A2

Natural Legacy Seeds, R.R. 2, C-1 Laird, Armstrong, BC V0E 1B0
(has unusual grasses)

And don't neglect to look at the seed exchanges most plant societies and garden societies have each December. This is an inexpensive way to get unusual and interesting seeds that you won't find anywhere else.

# Index